DINOSAURS ALIVE AND WELL!

◇ A Guide to Good Health ◇

Laurie Krasny Brown ◇ Marc Brown

Little, Brown and Company

Boston Toronto London

With love to Helen Brauner,
my spirited, energetic mother.
— L.K.B.

Your enthusiasm for life makes
you one terrific mother-in-law.
— M.B.

Our special thanks to Dr. Jane Gardner, Assistant Professor of Maternal and Child Health, Harvard School of Public Health; Dr. Norine Johnson, Clinical Psychologist; Albert Kimball, Principal of the William L. Foster School; Roger Paine, Director of Interface, and Dr. Leonard Rappaport, Director of the Medical Diagnostic Program at Children's Hospital in Boston.

Copyright © 1990 by Laurie Krasny Brown and Marc Brown

First Edition

Library of Congress Cataloging-in-Publication Data
Brown, Laurene Krasny.
    Dinosaurs alive and well: a guide to good health / Laurie Krasny Brown and Marc Brown.
        p.   cm.
    Summary: Presents, in simple text and illustrations, advice on nutrition, exercise, relationships with friends and family, and ways of dealing with stress.
    ISBN 0-316-10998-3
    1. Children — Health and hygiene — Juvenile literature.
[1. Health.] I. Brown, Marc Tolon. II. Title.
RA777.B76   1990
613'.0432 — dc20   89-37182
                                                            CIP
                                                            AC

10 9 8 7 6 5 4 3 2

WOR

Joy Street Books are published by
Little, Brown and Company (Inc.).

Published simultaneously in Canada
by Little, Brown & Company (Canada) Limited

Printed in the United States of America

◇ Contents ◇

Take Care of Yourself

There's just one you.
That makes you special.
There's a lot you can do to take care of yourself
and become the healthiest, happiest person you can be!

Taking care of yourself means treating yourself well every single day — looking out for your body, your mind, and your spirit.

All your energy comes from what you eat. The more active you are, the more energy, or calories, you use. One banana gives you enough energy to sleep for an hour and a half but to bicycle for only ten minutes.

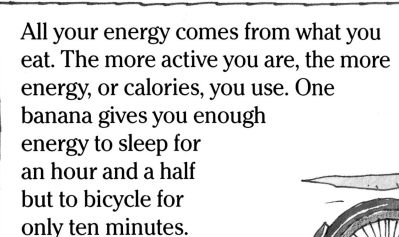

Good energy foods are

Your body can use this energy right away, and it lasts a long time.

Candy, soda, and other sugary snacks give you quick energy too, but soon leave you feeling weak and hungry again.

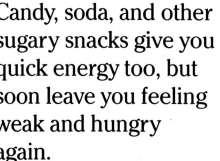

Too many fats and oils like those in bacon, butter, and hot dogs can make *you* fat and slow you down.

Food also provides the raw materials your body needs to grow.

Your body needs thirteen different vitamins. Each does a special job. Vitamin A helps your eyes adjust to the dark.
Vitamin C helps your skin heal and helps prevent colds and other illnesses.

The protein in food helps keep your muscles firm. It helps build healthy hair and blood, too. Don't pass up:

MILK

NUTS

You can get all the vitamins you need from food — especially fresh fruits and vegetables or cereal. If you're looking for a snack, remember: fruit gives you more vitamins than cookies or cake!

About twenty different minerals also help to keep you going.
Two of the most important are:

Calcium
It helps build strong bones and teeth. You'll find it in milk, cheese, yogurt, and ice cream.

Iron
Having enough iron helps keep you from feeling tired all the time. Eggs, beans, cereal, and liver are all good iron foods.

Fiber is the "rough stuff" in foods like fruit, vegetables, and whole-wheat bread. It helps you digest what you eat.

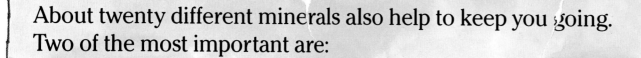

Do you know that your body is mostly water? You can't live without it, so drink as much as you can. And guess what: fruit and vegetables have lots of water in them, too!

Your body needs some fat to protect bones and organs and to keep you warm. But being overweight slows you down and makes your heart work too hard.

One way you get too fat is by eating too much, so before you take that next bite, stop and think: Am I *really* hungry?

Breakfast is the most important meal of the day. After going all night without food, your body is like a car with an empty gas tank. You need to fill up before you can go very far.

The best way to feed yourself is to eat regular meals and to eat all kinds of different foods — the fresher the better.

Suit Yourself

Clothes aren't just for show; they also protect your body from all kinds of weather.

The best way to stay warm is to dress in layers. Air caught between the layers helps retain your body heat. If you get hot, just take off a layer.

Wearing a hat makes you feel warm all over. Without one you lose a lot of body heat through your head. Try it and see!

On warm days, loose, lightweight clothes are best. They let air move closer to your body and cool it off.

Wearing light colors also helps you stay cool. They reflect sun rays instead of soaking them up.

The sun can burn your skin, especially in the middle of the day when its rays are strongest. Don't forget sunscreen and a hat to shade your eyes!

TAR PITS PARK

Think of shoes as friends for your feet. They cushion when you run, grip when you climb, keep out rain or snow, and help toes stay warm.

Feeling good outside can help you feel good inside. If you're feeling sad, try wearing your favorite color or outfit — it just might cheer you up!

Clothes can prepare you for any occasion. Well, *almost* any occasion.

WASH UP

Why bother to stay clean? You not only look better but stay healthier. Germs like bacteria and viruses can make you sick, so why not wash them away?

Hair
Use mild shampoo to wash out dirt and grease. Dry with a towel. Then gently comb or brush.

Face
Wash every day with soap and water. Natural oils in your skin trap dirt. Soapy water dissolves oils and lets dirt slide off easily.

Teeth
Clean at least twice a

day, especially after eating meals and snacks. Brush with fluoride toothpaste and gently pull dental floss up and down between teeth to get rid of food left behind.

Hands

Lather up with soap and water before eating, after using the toilet, and whenever they're dirty.

Fingernails

Scrub with a brush. Try not to bite: it weakens nails, and dirt from under them ends up in your mouth.

Shower or bathe your whole body often. It feels good to be clean!

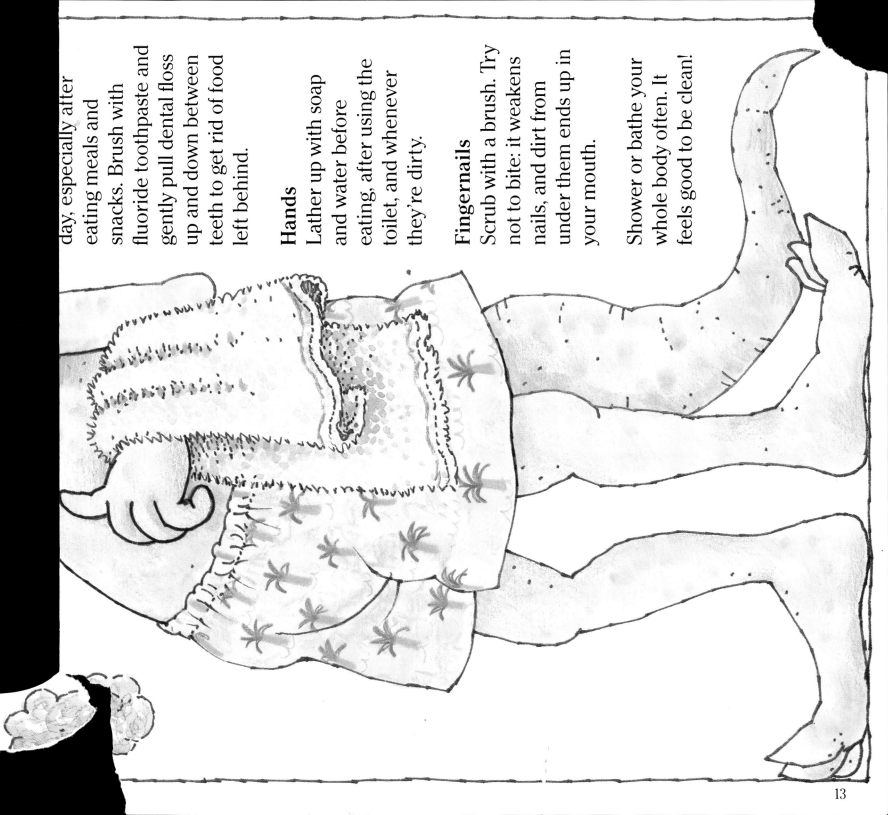

Exercise Your Body

Exercising every day helps your body stay healthy. When you exercise, your body works harder, your heartbeat is stronger, and you can feel your pulse go faster. Even though it takes energy to exercise, getting exercise helps you feel *more* energetic.

Some exercises make you stronger. Muscles that get no exercise become weak and flabby. They may even shrink in size.

Other exercises help your body stay flexible.

And, the more you exercise, the longer you'll be able to play without getting tired.

There are many different games and sports. The only way to find out which ones you like is to try them!

Some sports take lots of practice. Try to remember: you don't have to be perfect at a sport to have fun.

Everyone's body is different. Don't worry about what yours can't do — be proud of what you *can* do!

Exercise Your Mind

Your body isn't all that needs exercise —
so does your mind. Every time you
pretend, make decisions, figure
something out, or learn something new,
you're exercising your mind. It doesn't
happen only in school!

Believe in yourself! Expecting that you can do something is often half the battle.

You may want to do things the same way your friends do, but it's good to think for yourself, too.

Always doing the same thing can put your mind to sleep.

Everyone is good at something. Trying different activities helps you discover your own special talents.

Deal with Your Feelings

Feelings aren't right or wrong — they just are. Sometimes we all feel . . .

mad

sad

scared

glad

Letting out your feelings is healthier than keeping them to yourself.

Don't sit and stew. Anger gives you energy to do all kinds of things!

mad

If you feel sad, crying helps you feel better.

sad

Sharing your scared feelings with someone you trust can help you feel less alone.

This test will be so hard!

I know it.

scared

Be proud of yourself when you do something well.

Mom, look! I won!

glad

Solving problems isn't always easy. But most problems can be solved if you look them right in the eye. And you'll usually feel better in the end.

mad Try to think up fair ways to settle arguments.

sad You can make a new friend after you lose an old one — when you're ready.

BIRDS FOR SALE

scared It takes courage to admit you're scared. But someone else's help may be just what you need.

Mrs. Silver, can you help me?

MATH BOOK

Don't Worry

Feeling tense and worried can give you aches and pains in your head or stomach. You are more likely to get sick or have accidents when you feel upset.

You don't have to just wait until you feel better. Getting out and exercising can help you shake off tense feelings.

Facing what's upsetting you also helps. Sometimes your imagination makes a problem seem worse than it really is.

Or try this.
First look for a quiet, peaceful place. Get comfortable so your muscles can relax.

Take deep breaths in and out through your nose. Concentrate on your breathing. Can you make it slow and even?

Next, tighten and then let go of different muscles one at a time: your arms, hands, legs, feet, and jaw. Let your whole body go as limp as a wet noodle.

Last, close your eyes. Pretend that your mind has a screen and *you* make the pictures. Imagine fun things like seeing yourself float on clouds.

Take It Easy

Remember that you don't always have to be busy.
Give yourself time to daydream and be by yourself.

Be a Friend, Have a Friend

There's nothing like a good friend to make you feel happy.

Being a friend means a lot of sharing.

Friends stick together through good and bad.

Give yourself time to get to know new friends — and give them time to get to know you.

Friends often like to do the same things or go to the same places.

But sometimes even friends want to do something different or to be by themselves. That's okay, too.

Because friends like each other just the way they are!

About Sneezes and Scrapes

No matter how well you take care of yourself, you're bound to get sick sometimes — everybody does. There's plenty *you* can do to help your body get better.

Take medicine only from parents or grown-ups you trust. If you feel worse after taking medicine, tell someone — you may be allergic to it.

Try not to spread germs to others! Cover your coughs and sneezes, throw tissues away, and wash your hands often.

Drinking lots of liquids washes germs out of your system and helps bring down any fever.

JUICE

SICK BOX

Getting extra rest gives your body a chance to fight off germs.

First-aid Tips

Washing cuts or scrapes with soap and warm water to remove dirt lowers the chance of infection.

A scab is a natural bandage that keeps germs out while new skin grows underneath. Don't pick it off! Be patient and let your cut heal by itself!

But it itches!

Cool off a minor burn with ice or cold water. Any blister that forms makes a perfect bandage while the skin heals.

To stop a nosebleed, sit quietly and pinch your nose firmly for at least three minutes. This gives your body time to form a blood clot.

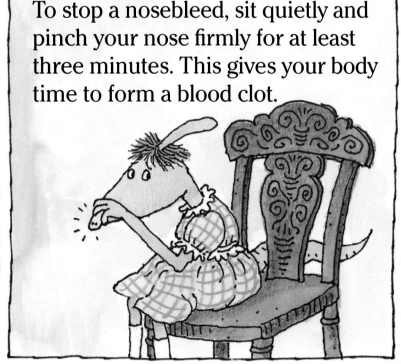

Help! From Grown-ups

As you get older, you do more and more things for yourself. But all sorts of grown-ups can still help you stay well and feel good about yourself. Don't be afraid to ask for help!

Parents

Teachers

Doctors

Relatives

Neighbors

Police

Religious Leaders

Baby-sitters

Time Out

Your body does a lot of work every day; it's no wonder it needs to rest at night! Rest helps clear your mind for the next day's activities.

Because you're still growing, you need more sleep than grown-ups — between ten and twelve hours each night.

If you don't get enough sleep, you're likely to feel grouchy or find it hard to concentrate the next day.

Help yourself to a good night's rest: let in a little fresh air and wear loose, comfortable sleeping clothes.

Relax before lights out: listen to quiet music or read a favorite story.

Be sure to tell someone if something is bothering you, so it doesn't keep you awake or give you nightmares.

Ask for a back rub or a hug — and give one, too!

Close your eyes and think about all the fun things you can do tomorrow.

Now that you know how to take care of yourself, you can help take care of others, too. You're part of the world of living things, each one special and unique . . . just like you!

DATE DUE			

BTSB Bound to Stay Bound Books, Inc.